KNITTING
FOR FUN!

By Jen Jones

Content Adviser: Stephanie Girard, Designer, Los Angeles, California

Reading Adviser: Frances J. Bonacci, Ed.D., Reading Specialist, Cambridge, Massachusetts

COMPASS POINT BOOKS

MINNEAPOLIS, MINNESOTA

Compass Point Books
3109 West 50th Street, #115
Minneapolis, MN 55410

Visit Compass Point Books on the Internet at www.compasspointbooks.com
or e-mail your request to custserv@compasspointbooks.com

Photographs ©: Creatas, front cover (left); Scott B. Rosen, front cover (right), 9, 15 (right), 17, 18, 19, 20, 21 (left), 22, 23, 24-25, 28-29, 30-31, 32-33, 34, 35; Digital Vision, 4-5; AP Wide World Photos, 7, 12-13, 21 (right), 40-41, 45 (bottom left); Istockphoto, 8-9, 15 (left), 47; Shutterstock, 10-11, 26-27, 38-39 (right inset, bottom); Photos.com, 36-37, 42 (top left, top, right), 45 (top, bottom right); Photodisc, 42 (bottom), 43 (left); Ingram Publishing, 43 (center, right), 44

Illustrator: Antoine Clarke/Bill SMITH STUDIO
Artist: Stefanie Girard

Editors: Deb Berry and Aubrey Whitten/Bill SMITH STUDIO; and Shelly Lyons
Designer/Page Production: Geron Hoy, Kavita Ramchandran, Sinae Sohn, Marina Terletsky, and Brock Waldron/Bill SMITH STUDIO
Photo Researcher: Jacqueline Lissy Brustein, Scott Rosen, and Allison Smith/Bill SMITH STUDIO
Art Director: Jaime Martens
Creative Director: Keith Griffin
Editorial Director: Carol Jones
Managing Editor: Catherine Neitge

Library of Congress Cataloging-in-Publication Data
Jones, Jen, 1976-
Knitting for fun! / By Jen Jones.
        p. cm.— (For fun!)
Includes bibliographical references and index.
ISBN 0-7565-1681-1 (hard cover)
1. Knitting—Patterns. I. Title. II. Series.
TT820.J62 2005
746.43'2—dc22

                                              2005030282

Table of Contents

The Basics

Doing It

People, Places, and Fun

Note: In this book, there are two kinds of vocabulary words. Knitting Words to Know are words specific to knitting. They are defined on page 46. Other Words to Know are helpful words that aren't related only to knitting. They are on page 47.

Knitting Know-How

You probably have a favorite knit sweater or scarf, perhaps something you bought or got as a present. But have you ever thought about knitting something yourself? Now is the time to learn. Knitting has become a hip hobby for people of all ages. If you'd like to create your own clothes and accessories, this book will help you get in on the fun and learn knitting.

Taking up knitting is a great way to exercise your creativity. From scarves to bags to sweaters, your closet will be bursting at the seams with one-of-a-kind designs. Knitting is relaxing and is something fun to do by yourself or with others.

Learning to knit doesn't happen overnight. It takes time to master the different stitching methods and techniques. As you improve, you'll begin to experiment with types of yarn and needles, but it's best to start simple.

Knitting Through the Years

Knitting has been in practice for thousands of years, although its exact time of origin is not known. Most fabrics are not built to last hundreds of years, so there are very few ancient knitting relics. However, many historians believe knitting began in Egypt, where knitted socks were discovered in tombs that dated back to 1300.

Until William Lee invented the knitting machine in 1589, many men and women made a living knitting garments. During this time, numerous knitting guilds existed in which men would go through apprentice training to become skilled knitters. However, after the introduction of the machinery, knitting turned into a personal pastime.

Down Time

Knitting was especially popular during times of war, when citizens rallied to provide clothing for soldiers. During the 18th, 19th, and 20th centuries, towns held knitting contests to see who could produce the most for those in need.

Knitting wasn't always popular. In the 1980s, people strayed away from the age-old craft. Some think the rise of technology caused people to lose interest. However, today the number of people who enjoy knitting is at an all time high!

What You Need to Start

Just like artists use a paintbrush and canvas, knitters rely on trusty tools to create their masterpieces. Before starting your projects, you'll need to stock up on the necessary materials and equipment.

Shopping List

- Yarn
- Scissors
- Knitting needles
- Pins
- Tape measure
- Markers

Here are a few tools that you might not have heard of:

- A **crochet hook** saves the day when you need to pick up dropped stitches or take care of loose ends.

- **Point protectors** are handy devices that keep stitches in place when you're not working on your project.

- A **row counter** is placed on the end of your knitting needle to keep track of how many rows you've already created.

- Shaped like a giant safety pin, the **stitch holder** is used to keep stitches, other than the ones you are currently working on, from coming undone.

- You can spot a **yarn needle** because it has a large hole on one end and a blunt tip on the other. Often referred to as a "tapestry needle," it's used for embroidery and other finishing touches.

Having a Ball

Yarn is the key ingredient for any knitting project. It comes in different colors as well as textures, weights, and fibers.

Fibers are either natural (from plants or animals) or synthetic (man-made). The softness and feel of your final piece depends on the fiber you choose. Examples of natural fibers are wool, silk, cotton, and cashmere. Synthetic fibers include polyester, nylon, and acrylic.

With the many yarns available for use, it's easy to get overwhelmed during the selection process. Clothing knitted from natural animal fibers will keep you warm. But before buying yarn, do a quick test by rubbing it against your skin to make sure you're not allergic. This test also allows you to see whether the finished product will feel comfortable or itchy.

The Inside Scoop On Yarn Labels

Reading yarn labels carefully is a must for new knitters. From the label (or "ball band"), you can find out which company made the yarn, the yarn's name and shade, and what fiber the yarn is made of. The label also provides needle size suggestions and proper care instructions.

Getting to the Point

If yarn is the canvas of knitting, needles are a knitter's paintbrushes. These are the main tools you will use to shape your yarn into something. Knitting needles come in different lengths and diameters and are made from steel, plastic, or wood.

Single-pointed needles have a point at one end and a knob on the other end, while double-pointed needles have points at both ends. Single-pointed needles are used to create flat fabric surfaces, and double-pointed needles are used for circular projects such as socks or gloves. More advanced knitters also use circular needles to create sweaters, blankets, and other large items.

Dealing With Diameter

A general rule is to use thinner needles for thin yarn and thicker needles for thick yarn. Although diameter can range from zero to 19, needles with diameter sizes from six to 10 are recommended for beginners.

10

8

6

Ready, Set, Knit!

Knitting is the act of joining stitches, or loops of yarn, in rows that will ultimately become fabric. Once you learn the basics, you can create everything from sweaters to socks.

Whether you are left-handed or right-handed will affect the way you create your stitches. Right-handed people usually use the English method, in which yarn is held in the right hand, whereas lefties use the opposite Continental method. (All of the knitting in this book is demonstrated using the English method.)

Get A Grip

Learning to hold your needles can be somewhat awkward until you gain more experience. Some knitters hold their needles like pencils, while others place their fingers near the tips of the needles. There are no rules, so do what feels most natural to you.

All Tied Up in Knots

The first step of any knitting project is making a slip knot. It is used to cast on the first stitches. Here is how to make a slip knot:

1. On your right hand, wrap the end of the yarn around your index and middle fingers. Hold the loop in place with your thumb.

2. With your left hand, pull the strand of yarn that is connected to the ball through the loop formed by your fingers.

3. Place the new loop on the needle and pull on both ends of the yarn to tighten the loop on the needle.

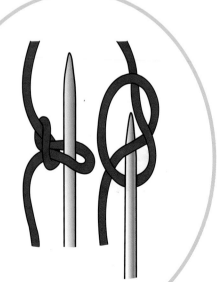

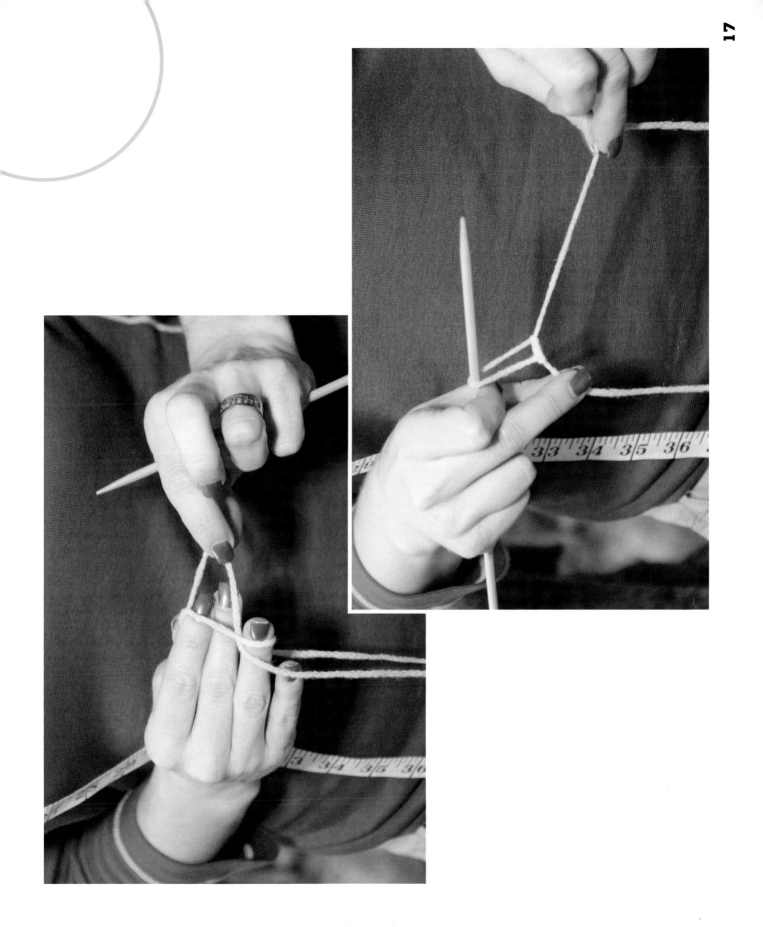

The First Row

Casting on is the process of creating your first row of stitches, which is the basis for any knitting project. Although there are several methods of casting on, this is the simplest:

1. Hold one needle with the slip knot in your right hand.

2. Wrap the yarn behind, then over your left thumb.

3. Insert the right needle underneath and through the yarn loop on your left thumb.

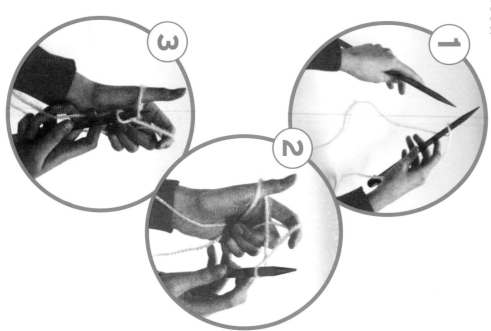

4. Go over the top of the yarn on your index finger, pull it through the loop, and remove your thumb.

5. Repeat these steps until you've made a row of stitches on the needle. Knitting patterns will tell you how many stitches to cast on per project.

Trusty Casting Tip

While casting on the first row, don't pull the stitches too tightly or it will be difficult to maneuver the needle through the yarn. You might even want to use a larger needle size to ensure loops that are easier to work with, then switch to smaller needles for the actual project.

Stitch Smarts for Beginners

Ihe knit stitch is the most basic knitting technique and can be used for a range of projects.

1. After you've cast on the first row of stitches, hold the needle with that row in your left hand and an empty needle in the right hand.

2. Insert the empty needle into the center of the first stitch so that the needles cross, with the right needle behind the left.

3. Wrap the yarn behind and around the right needle in a counterclockwise fashion.

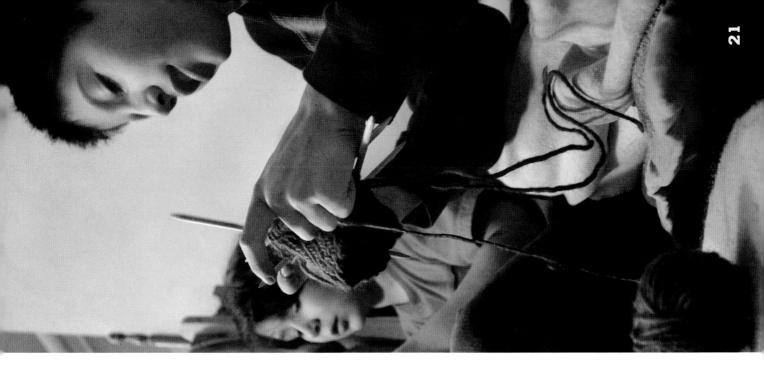

4. Hold the yarn in place with your right hand and guide the right needle toward you through the stitch you've just made.

5. Slip the stitch off the left needle, which will create a stitch on the right needle.

5. Continue to do this until all the stitches from your cast on row have been moved to the right needle.

Congratulations! You've successfully completed a row of knit stitches. If the first few attempts leave you scratching your head in confusion, don't be frustrated. It's normal to encounter some bumps in the road as you learn. Keep in mind that practice makes perfect.

Endings and Beginnings

It's important to know how to properly remove, or bind off, the stitches. Otherwise, you'll be stuck with an unraveled mess and nothing to show for your hard work.

Joining Up:

If you're not completely done with your creation but need more yarn, then you need to join your work up with a new ball.

1. Start with a new stitch.

2. Wrap the yarn from the new ball behind and around the right needle in a counterclockwise fashion.

3. Continue to knit the row using the new yarn to make your stitches.

Binding Off:

1. When you are ready to bind off, you'll need to make a final row. Start by knitting two stitches.

2. Insert the left needle into the first stitch you made on the right needle.

3. Move this stitch over the second stitch and lift it off the right needle. (There should be one stitch left.)

4. Knit another stitch, then keep repeating steps two and three until only one stitch is left on the right needle.

5. Cut the yarn, leaving a 6-inch (15-cm) tail. Pull that tail through the final stitch, remove the needle, and tighten the yarn.

Plus and Minus

What if you want your knitting to take a shape other than square or rectangular? You'll need to learn how to increase and decrease your stitches.

Increasing stitches is a method used in making a garment wider. To do so, a knitter makes two stitches out of one, which is called a bar increase:

1. Knit into the stitch to be increased, without dropping it off of the left needle.

2. Insert the right needle into the back of that same stitch on the left needle.

3. Knit the stitch again, which will create two stitches on the right needle.

4. Slip the stitch off of the left needle. Your stitch is now officially plus one.

Decreasing your stitches creates the opposite effect by narrowing your garment. The most basic decreasing method is to knit two together (or K2Tog), which decreases your knitting by one stitch:

1. Insert the right needle into the next two stitches on the left needle.

2. Knit those two stitches together as if they were one stitch. This decreases by one stitch.

Trusty Tip

Stitch markers can be helpful tools when increasing and decreasing more complex patterns.

Master the Methods

On the following pages, you'll sharpen your skills with some funky, fun projects that will be the crowning glory of your closet! Before you can begin, you'll need to learn the following terms and techniques:

Garter Stitches: rows of knit stitches.

Purl Stitches: are commonly used and are considered to be a backward version of the knit stitch.

Stockinette Stitch: a combination of knit and purl stitches, resulting in a V-shaped pattern. To create a stockinette effect, simply cast on a row of stitches, then alternate rows with knit and purl stitches. (Knit row 1, purl row 2, knit row 3, etc.) Purling is easy. Follow the directions below.

1. After you've cast on the first row of stitches, hold the needle with that row in your left hand and an empty needle in your right hand. Make sure the yarn is in front.

2. Insert the right needle into the first stitch of the left needle, from right to left. (The right needle should end up in front of the left needle.)

3. Wrap the yarn around the tip of the right needle, from right to left.

4. Slip the stitch off the left needle by lowering the right needle, making sure to keep the new stitch on the right needle. Continue doing so with all stitches until they have all been moved to the right needle.

Flip-Flops

Calling all tired tootsies! Want to go for a walk in the clouds? These comfy flip-flops will make you feel like you're walking on air.

Shopping List

- U.S. size 8 needles
- Eyelash yarn or fun fur
- 1 pair of flip-flops
- Safety pins
- Yarn needle
- Wiggly eyes or buttons

Technique: Garter Stitch

1. Cast on 12 stitches.

2. Knit every row until you have a length that covers your flip-flop, using the garter stitch method.

3. Bind off.

4. Leave a 2-foot (60-cm) tail of yarn.

5. Make another strip for the other flip-flop.

6. Fold the strip of knitting in half and mark the center with a safety pin.

7. Secure the center of the knitted strip to the center of the flip-flop strap with a safety pin. The safety pin will keep your knit pieces on the flip-flop when you're done.

8. Wrap the strip around the flip-flop strap and stitch the sides together.

9. Wrap both ends of the yarn firmly at the back base of the straps and weave back in the ends.

10. Decorate your finished product with wiggly eyes or pretty buttons.

Tech Tote

What's a girl or boy to do with too many gadgets? Knit a trusty tote. This handy holder can help you carry your MP3 player or cell phone from place to place.

Shopping List

- Four colors of suede yarn
- U.S. size 9 needles
- Yarn needle

Technique: Stockinette Stitch, Color Changing

To make the body of the tote:

1. Cast on 48 stitches.

2. Knit 9 rows in stockinette stitch (Knit 1 row, purl 1 row) with color A.

3. Knit 3 rows in stockinette stitch with color B.

4. Knit 5 rows in stockinette stitch with color C.

5. Knit 3 rows in stockinette stitch with color D.

6. Bind off.

7. Weave in the ends.

8. Fold in half and stitch up the bottom and side.

To make the strap:

1. Cast on three stitches.

2. Knit 45 rows in stockinette stitch.

3. Bind off.

4. With each tail, stitch the strap to the body of the tote at one top corner and weave in the ends.

Trusty Tip

To attach the tote to your jeans, slip the strap through your belt loop and then slide the tote through the strap's loop. Place your gadget in the tote and you're all set.

Pocket Scarf

Winter, be warned! This handy scarf does double duty by keeping both your hands and neck warm. Get ready for the fall and winter sports season by using the colors of your favorite football or hockey teams, or your school colors.

Shopping List

- Thick yarn
- U.S. size 17 needles
- Yarn needle

Technique: Basket Weave Stitch

1. Cast on nine stitches.

2. Make sure to bring your yarn to the front for purl stitches and to the back for knit stitches.

   - Row 1: knit 3, purl 3, knit 3
   - Row 2: purl 3, knit 3, purl 3
   - Row 3: knit 3, purl 3, knit 3
   - Row 4: knit 3, purl 3, knit 3
   - Row 5: purl 3, knit 3, purl 3
   - Row 6: knit 3, purl 3, knit 3

3. Continue by repeating rows one through six until you have the desired length scarf with enough to fold up on one or both ends to make a pocket.

4. Bind off.

5. Use the tails to seam up one side of the pocket and weave in the ends.

6. Cut a 2-foot length of yarn to seam up the other side of the pocket.

Sweat Bands

Jazz up any workout outfit with these hip sweatbands. You'll be the talk of gym class with these cool cuffs.

Shopping List

- Two colors of yarn
- Size 4 needles
- Yarn needle

Skills/Techniques

We'll be increasing and decreasing. Increase is abbreviated as "1Inc" and decrease is abbreviated is "K2Tog."

1. Cast on 13 stitches with color A:

- Row 1: purl
- Row 2: knit 1Inc, knit to last 2 stitches, K2Tog
- Row 3: purl
- Row 4: knit 1Inc, knit to last 2 stitches, K2Tog

2. Repeat rows one through four with color B.

3. Alternate this way until you have a strip big enough to stretch over your hand and fit on your wrist.

4. Bind off.

5. Sew the two ends together and weave in the ends.

Knitting All Over the World

The popularity and impact of knitting reaches the entire world. Some countries rely on different types of yarn fibers as a major export. New Zealand contributes 25 percent of the world's wool thanks to its large sheep population. (There are 12 sheep for every one person!) Egypt is known for its production of luxurious cotton, while Mongolia is renowned for fine cashmere.

Different areas of the world are noted for utilizing unique types of stitching. Ireland's knitters have used cable stitching to make fishing sweaters out of wool. Scandinavian knitters create socks, sweaters, and hats with the damask knitting method.

Cable knit sweaters, hats, scarves, and gloves will keep you extra warm in cold weather.

Real-Life Knitting

Whether it's done by hand or machine, knitting is the source of many of the clothes in your closet. Look at the labels of your favorite shirts or pants; you'll see that many of them are composed of knitted rayon, cotton, or other fibers. While much of the clothing sold at big department stores is knitted by machine, hand-knit clothes are likely to be found at smaller boutiques and craft shows. (Machines are used to produce a large volume of clothing, whereas hand-knit clothes are usually one-of-a-kind.)

If you want to design your own clothing, it's smart to take a cue from fashion experts. Knitting magazines often provide original patterns from well-known designers who follow the latest trends and styles. You can also find free patterns online for just about any type of clothing or accessory you want to make, from shawls to skirts to sweats. Follow the patterns or make them your own with funky variations. The sky's the limit!

Friends Who Knit Together

Love knitting? Join the club, literally! In small towns and big cities, knitting clubs exist for those who want to practice their hobby in the company of old and new friends while learning new techniques and sharing ideas. You might want to check with your local library or community center to see if there is a club that meets regularly.

If you'd rather start a club, school is a great place to begin. Recruit fellow knitters and put flyers up in the hallways. After you've got a solid membership base, inquire with school officials to see if they will let you use an empty classroom for your meetings.

Being part of a knitting club is great because it gives you reasons and time to do what you love. Plus, many stores offer discounts to students or knitting club members. All you have to do is ask.

Stitching To Help

Knitting groups often use their collective power to do good works in the community. Donating finished products to the homeless, nursing homes, and hospitals can be a wonderful way to help others with your hobby.

What Happend When?

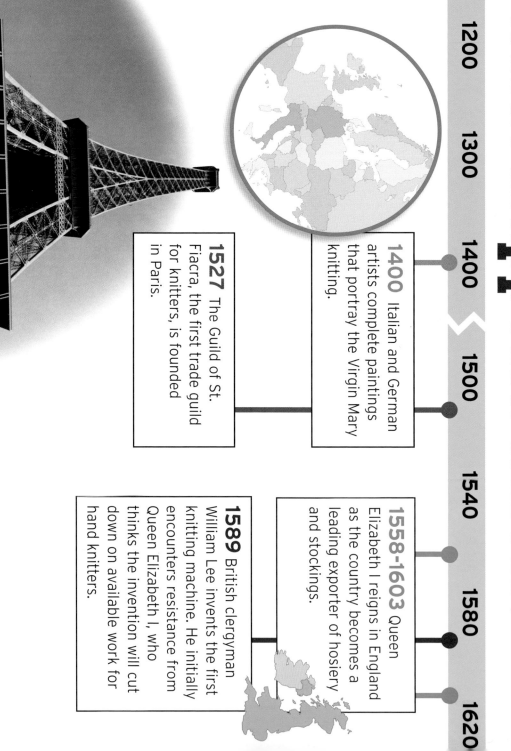

| 1200 | 1300 | 1400 | 1500 | 1540 | 1580 | 1620 |

1400 Italian and German artists complete paintings that portray the Virgin Mary knitting.

1527 The Guild of St. Fiacra, the first trade guild for knitters, is founded in Paris.

1558-1603 Queen Elizabeth I reigns in England as the country becomes a leading exporter of hosiery and stockings.

1589 British clergyman William Lee invents the first knitting machine. He initially encounters resistance from Queen Elizabeth I, who thinks the invention will cut down on available work for hand knitters.

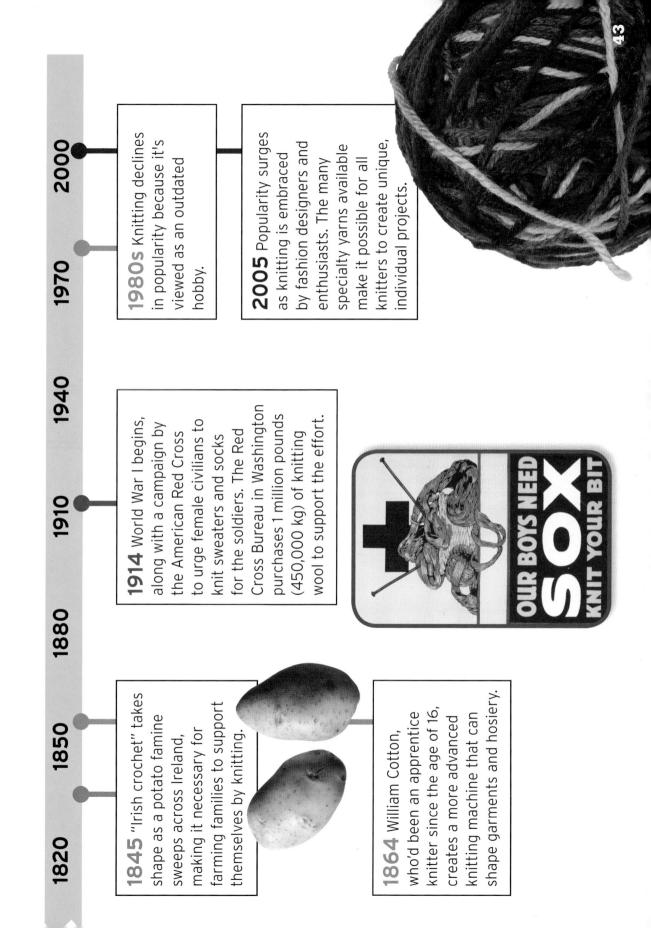

1820 1850 1880 1910 1940 1970 2000

1845 "Irish crochet" takes shape as a potato famine sweeps across Ireland, making it necessary for farming families to support themselves by knitting.

1864 William Cotton, who'd been an apprentice knitter since the age of 16, creates a more advanced knitting machine that can shape garments and hosiery.

1914 World War I begins, along with a campaign by the American Red Cross to urge female civilians to knit sweaters and socks for the soldiers. The Red Cross Bureau in Washington purchases 1 million pounds (450,000 kg) of knitting wool to support the effort.

1980s Knitting declines in popularity because it's viewed as an outdated hobby.

2005 Popularity surges as knitting is embraced by fashion designers and enthusiasts. The many specialty yarns available make it possible for all knitters to create unique, individual projects.

OUR BOYS NEED SOX KNIT YOUR BIT

Fun Knitting Facts

Many years ago, knitters used rhymes to help them remember the complicated handiwork. These rhymes are still used when teaching beginners how to knit. One such rhyme refers to the knit stitch: "In the front door, around the back, out through the window, and off jumps Jack."

In 1589, Reverend William Lee, from England, invented the first knitting machine. He invented it to get the attention of a woman who was an avid knitter.

Cashmere, a natural fiber yarn, comes from cashmere goats. Mohair comes from angora goats.

In the 1890s, college athletes came up with a new slang term: sweaters. The word described those heavy perspiration-causing wool tops they wore for competitive sports.

According to the Craft Yarn Council, more than 38 million women in the United States know how to knit. Celebrities, like Julia Roberts, Cameron Diaz, Sarah Jessica Parker, and Madonna also know how to knit.

Knitting Words to Know

acrylic: a synthetic fiber that is inexpensive and easy to wash

ball band: other words for "yarn label"

cashmere: an expensive natural fiber well-known for its qualities of luxury and softness

cast on: to create the first row of stitches on a knitting needle

Continental method: a knitting method in which the left hand holds the working yarn

cotton: a natural, lightweight fiber

crochet hook: used for picking up dropped stitches or creating garments with fringe

English method: a knitting method in which the right hand holds the working yarn

nylon: a strong, synthetic fiber that is often blended with other fibers

pattern: a set of instructions for knitting and completing a garment or project

polyester: a synthetic fiber that is inexpensive and virtually wrinkle-free

point protector: protective devices used to keep stitches in place during down time

row counter: a device that lets knitters manually keep track of how many rows they've completed

silk: a natural fiber that is spun by silkworms and has a smooth texture

stitch holder: a device that maintains the shape of areas of the knitting project that are not being worked on

weight: the thickness of the yarn, which can range from fine to bulky

wool: an inexpensive, natural fiber that is known for its warmth

yarn needle: used for embroidery and weaving in loose ends of yarn

Other Words to Know

guild: an association of people who practice the same craft

relic: an ancient keepsake or artifact

synthetic: produced by chemicals

tapestry: a large, decorative cloth

Where To Learn More

AT THE LIBRARY

Abrams, Carol, Maureen Lasher and Jennifer Wenger. *Teen Knitting Club: Chill Out and Knit.* New York: Workman Publishing, Inc., 2004.

Clewer, Carolyn. *Kids Can Knit.* Hauppage, NY: Quarto Inc., 2003.

Vogue Knitting. *Beginner Basics On the Go!* New York: Sixth & Spring Books, 2003.

ON THE ROAD

The Textile Museum
2320 S St. N.W.
Washington, DC 20008
202/667-0441

ON THE WEB

For more information on this topic, use FactHound.

1. Go to *www.facthound.com*
2. Type in this book ID: 0756516811
3. Click on the *Fetch It* button.

FactHound will find the best Web sites for you.

ABOUT THE AUTHOR

Jen Jones is a Los Angeles-based writer who has published stories in magazines. She has written for E! Online and PBS Kids, and is a website producer.

INDEX